MAKE
BARRETTES

16 Projects for Creating Beautiful Hair Accessories

& MORE

QUARRY BOOKS
Rockport, Massachusetts
Distributed by North Light Books
Cincinnati, Ohio

First published in the United States of America by
Quarry Books, an imprint of Rockport Publishers, Inc.
146 Granite Street
Rockport, Massachusetts 01966-1299
Telephone: (508) 546-9590
Fax: (508) 546-7141

Distributed to the book trade and art trade
in the United States of America by
North Light, an imprint of F & W Publications
1507 Dana Avenue
Cincinnati, Ohio 45207
Telephone: (800) 289-0963

Other Distribution by
Rockport Publishers, Inc.
Rockport, Massachusetts 01966-1299

ISBN: 1-56496-285-7

10   9   8   7   6   5   4   3   2   1

Designer: Laura Herrmann Design
Photography: Paul Forrester

Printed in Hong Kong
by Regent Publishing Services Limited

CONTENTS

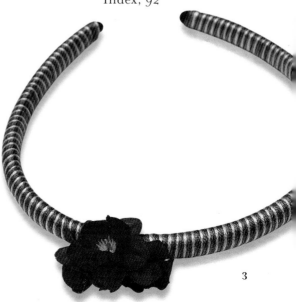

3

BARRETTE BASICS

YOU DON'T HAVE TO BE A HIGHLY SKILLED PROFESSIONAL to create beautiful clips, combs, headbands, and hair slides. With just a little imagination and the right materials and tools, you can produce wonderful works of art from classic basic elements such as beads, precious metals, and simple barrette bases. Or you can transform mundane, household items such as buttons, fabric scraps, and newspapers into sophisticated hair accessories.

Materials

To make fabulous hair ornaments, there are a few basic materials you will need in your craft box. The first and most important are the right bases. Metal clip-fastening bases and plain white plastic headbands are available ready to decorate in any way you choose from craft or jewelry suppliers. You can also transform inexpensive headbands, clips, or hair combs bought at a local drugstore or department store, using a wide variety of different decorative effects.

Synthetic polymer clays can also be used to make spectacular beads and bases for clips and hair slides in every shape imaginable. Fired in a low-temperature domestic oven and then varnished, polymer clays can imitate some of the finest ceramics. They come in a fantastic range of colors that can be used alone, twisted together in various color combinations to create wonderful marbled effects, or built up into imitation millefiori canes for barrette bases or bead decoration.

Paper is suitable for any form of craft work and jewelry design is no exception. Use papier-mâché techniques to cover simple cardboard base shapes with newspaper to make stylish barrettes. Take advantage of the wide selection of decorative paper available and add a colorful, patterned finishing layer to a plain papier-mâché base. Roll colorful paper into paper bead charms to hang from a barrette base or glue to a cardboard base.

Beads, a basic component in making necklaces, bracelets, pins, and earrings, can also be used to make striking barrettes. With a ball of plasticine as the base, make papier-mâché beads that can be decorated in your own style or painted to mimic real beads.

The basic elements used for making hair accessories in this book include *hair clips, hair combs, headbands,* and *hair slides,* which can be purchased at craft stores, drugstores, or department stores, and become the start of fabulous designs.

The Elements of Style

HAIR CLIPS from jewelry suppliers come in a selection of sizes—the smaller ones can be used to hold sections of hair in place while the larger ones will secure a ponytail or chignon. You can glue fabulous faux jewel stones, papier-mâché, or polymer clay shapes of your own design to the base or secure strings of beads through the preformed holes. Ready-made store-bought clips in imitation tortoiseshell, plain plastic, or padded fabric can also be decorated in a variety of ways, including painting, adding beads or even silk flowers.

HAIR COMBS are available with plain or intricately designed tops and come in a variety of sizes to suit different styles and thicknesses of hair. These are easy to find in local stores, and large quantities can be bought from wholesalers. Combs can be wrapped with ribbons or thread, decorated with glittering jewels, or wired with sprays of fake flowers.

Other Elements

HEADBANDS are sold by many craft and jewelry suppliers in different sizes, widths, and textures. These can be painted, covered with colorful embroidery threads, luxurious braids, and even pasted strips of newspaper—mix PVA glue with the wallpaper paste to give the finished piece a degree of flexibility. You can also encase them in fabulous fabrics that can be gathered to create interesting finished effects. Store-bought padded bands look wonderful wrapped with strings of exotic beads or decorated with jazzy jewels glued in place with adhesive.

HAIR SLIDES are easy to make using fabric scraps, polymer clays, and fine sheet metals. Make your own pins from wooden skewers or look for more original ideas like brightly-colored plastic needles, knitting row markers and cable needles, or thick jeweler's wire wrought into shape. You can also use richly embroidered plastic canvas (cut holes to take the pin before working the embroidery) and even papier-mâché techniques to create totally original designs.

Basic Tools & Adhesives

All of the projects in this book are easy to make and require little space for their creation—most can be put together at the kitchen table with only the basic tools. Lay down a craft board to protect the table, and provide a flat, even surface to work on. A self-healing cutting mat, marked with ruled lines, makes it easy to draw and cut shapes and is useful for working with metal. Organize your bases and decorative elements in boxes and trays.

Use a craft knife for making precise cuts and tin cutters for cutting metals. For measuring and cutting perfect straight lines, a steel ruler is more practical than plastic as it won't be damaged by a craft knife. A tape measure is essential for measuring curved surfaces such as headbands.

Other useful tools include a blunt needle, a fine bradawl, and a single hole punch for making holes in hard materials. Use toothpicks or basic wooden kebab skewers for softer materials like polymer clays. Tweezers and toothpicks help to hold and glue small jewels and beads in place. Attach a small clamp or clothespin to hold items together while the glue sets. Metal files are useful if you prefer working with sheet tin, copper, or pewter, but are not essential for other materials where the rougher side of an emery board will work just as well.

Round-nosed and needle-nosed pliers, available from craft and jewelry specialists, clamp shaped jewel stones into their mounts and hold awkward shapes. Use round-nosed pliers to turn loops in head or eye pins, and to twist and coil jeweler's wire into shape. Squeeze calotte crimps together and flatten joints with needle-nosed pliers. Use two pairs of pliers to open and close jump rings. Buy them with integral wire cutters or invest in a separate pair of wire cutters for trimming head and eye pins, and jeweler's wire.

As a general rule, an all-purpose, clear-drying glue and a stronger, bonding epoxy glue are all you will need to ensure that your wonderful design won't break when you wear it. Take the time to read and follow the directions on the glue container. Use common sense: make sure that barrette surfaces are clean and grease-free; and, with some glues, you may need to work in a well-ventilated room.

Lightly scuff plastic surfaces with an emery board before gluing to

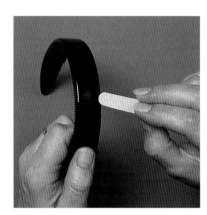

provide a surface the object can adhere to. Make sure surfaces are dust-free before gluing. Use just

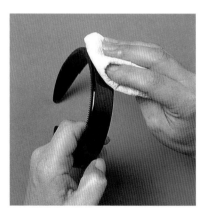

as much glue as you need for each project—too much glue will cause it to ooze out, marring the finished effect, and too little glue

will create a weak bond. Special pipettes and fine nozzled squeeze bottles make delivering the right amount of glue much easier; or squeeze a little

out into a dish or piece of cardboard and use a toothpick to apply it—a method that is especially useful when working with small jewel stones.

Tips & Techniques

To make surfaces clean and free of grease, use nail polish remover or rubbing alcohol on a lint-free cloth. Test a small area on a side that won't be seen, as some plastic surfaces can be damaged by the chemicals.

Basic Metalwork

Working with sheet metal creates a new world of design possibilities and is not as daunting as it seems—you don't need to have special skills or an expensive set of tools to create fabulous results.

Craft suppliers stock tin, aluminium, copper, and pewter in sheet form, which is easily cut and shaped using heavy duty scissors, tin cutters, or a craft knife. You can recycle materials such as soda cans and square olive oil cans as another alternative; make sure these are washed thoroughly, and then dried carefully to prevent rusting before starting your project.

Pressing a blunt needle, knitting needle, or ballpoint pen onto the metal will mark the outline of the shape to be cut. A self-healing rubber cutting mat is useful to work on as it keeps the metal from slipping as you mark the shape, and its surface has enough "give" to allow you to indent the metal easily. (Use a wad of newspaper if you don't have a cutting mat.) Other metalwork tools include fine hand files suitable for metal, a hammer and panel pin for creating pierced designs, and a steel ruler for marking straight lines.

To create *relief patterns,* make a tracing of your design and tape it over the metal shape. Work on a self-healing cutting mat or wad of newspapers,

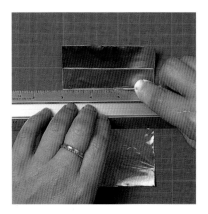

and use a tip of a knitting needle to trace the design onto the metal, pressing down firmly. Use a smooth action to create the best finish—stopping and starting in the middle of a line can create distortion. Wrap a piece of tape close to the end of the knitting needle to help prevent your fingers from slipping.

Pierced designs are easy to master and provide scope for creating a wide variety of different motifs. Draw your motif on paper and lay a piece of tracing paper on top. Transfer the design to the tracing paper by marking a dotted outline in pencil, making sure the dots are evenly spaced. Tape this to the metal and use the tip of a needle to make light indentations where the dots are to be placed. Remove the tracing paper and then use a hammer and panel pin to pierce the detail.

Textured finishes add a different dimension to designs and are easy to work on most soft metals.

For a hammered look, you can use anything from end of a paintbrush to a more professional ball-headed hammer. To prevent scratching the metal, wrap the head of the hammer with a piece of felt. Working on a different surface can also create varied finishes, so experiment first on metal scraps.

Polish the metal gently with a soft cloth to remove any greasy finger marks. Take care not to press too hard on relief designs as this can spoil the raised effect. File sharp edges smooth using a fine metal file or emery board. Backing the finished design with stiff cardboard, suede, or leather will give it more substance.

BASES FOR BARRETTES

SIMPLE FLAT-BACKED BASES FOR HAIR clips and hair slides are easy to make from polymer and air dry clays, papier-mâché shapes, and fabric scraps. These can then be decorated with paint effects, dazzling bead detail, or simple embroidery.

Making Simple Bases

The simplest bases can be shaped from polymer clays, which come in a range of colors. Knead the clay for several minutes with your hands to soften, then roll out flat, like pastry, to a depth of approximately ¼ to ⅜ inch / .5 cm to 1 cm. Make sure the depth is uniform and has a smooth surface without air bubbles or cracks, then cut out the shape you require. You can use cookie cutters or, with a cardboard template of your own design, cut out the shape carefully using a craft knife.

For a three-dimensional effect, layer clay shapes on top of each other. Press them with objects such as a perforated fitting or fallen leaves to create a textured finish. Design a glittering jewel-encrusted finish by pressing glass beads or flat-backed jewel stones into the surface—glass will not melt when the clay is fired. If you are working with several colors, be careful to keep your hands clean to avoid mixing the colors. Use acrylic paints or jewel stones to disguise any faults (water-based colors separate on the polymer base).

Cardboard shapes layered with pasted strips of newspaper, a basic papier-mâché technique, can also become simple clip bases perfect for painting and decorating with fabric scraps, braids, or sequins. Create textured finishes by gluing string or paper pulp in pretty patterns to the base shape, or add jewel stones for a touch of glamour.

Decorate these bases with beads, charms, or drops by inserting eye pins or piercing holes at the relevant points. Hang just one beautiful jewel from the center bottom of the design or dangle several beaded strands. To attach such findings, trim an eye pin to size (approximately ¼ to ⅜ inch / .5 cm to 1 cm, depending on the size of the design) and insert it into the edge of a clay or papier-mâché design before it is set. Dab a bit of glue to secure it once it is rigid. Then join wired single beads or groups of beads directly or with a jump ring to the eye pin.

DECORATIVE EFFECTS

BEADS, A BASIC COMPONENT IN JEWELRY MAKING SINCE THE BEGINNING of time, are ideal for creating unique decorative effects on many hair ornaments. Look for smaller beads, which are more suited for embroidery work than for making necklaces. Use them to highlight patterns on decorative braids or to add a glittering finish to ribbon-wrapped combs and bands.

Jewel stones add instant glamour to most pieces of jewelry. Buy them with flat backs, which are easy to glue in position, or cut like genuine precious stones, which must be set in special metal mounts. These stones are made from acrylic or glass and come in a range of sizes, some with holes to allow them to be sewn in place. Both types have mirrored backs and care needs to be taken when handling them as the mirror finish can easily be scratched and spoil the finished effect.

Sequins come in an abundant array of sizes, colors, and shapes and can be sewn or glued directly to any type of hair accessory. Specialist craft and jewelry suppliers include most shapes in their catalogues; some even offer cheap bags of "sweepings"—sequins literally swept from the floor, cleaned, and bagged.

Synthetic polymer clay can be used to make the most spectacular bases in every shape and size imaginable. Fired in a domestic oven at low temperatures, they look like the finest ceramics, especially when varnished. They come in a fantastic range of colors that can be used on their own, or several different colors can be twisted together to create wonderful marbled effects. Once kneaded to soften and remove air bubbles, they can be rolled out like pastry and cut and shaped with a craft knife. Work intricate patterns into their surface by carefully adding different colored clays. Paint plain bases with subtle metallic paints to resemble precious metals.

Papier-mâché is one of the most versatile modeling mediums for any form of craft work and jewelry design is no exception. Using the most basic techniques you can cover simple cardboard shapes with newspaper to make stylish clips and hair slides. Take advantage of the sheer variety of decorative papers available today and use them as the finishing layer in papier-mâché or rolled into traditional paper bead shapes.

Found objects can be used to make fun, innovative hair jewelry and frequently cost nothing at all. Scraps of fabric, embroidery threads, and recycled cans are easy to transform into stylish designs. More unusual materials can be picked up on a visit to a flea market, rummage sale, or antique fair—old watches, broken up, can be used to decorate plain bases and transform something ordinary into a fun, unique design. Beads and flat-backed charms from other pieces of broken jewelry can be incorporated into creative hair decorations. Feathers from an unused feather duster or sterilized feathers found outdoors can also be used in your creations.

Transform unexciting hair accessories into something special by covering them with luxurious ribbons, rich textured braids, or colorful embroidery threads. These can be simply wrapped along the length of a headband or top of a hair comb—color coordinate one with a special outfit. To hold the ribbon or braid in place securely, place a blob of glue on the wrong side of a headband or comb close to one end, and position the thread or braid over the glue and hold in place while it dries using a small clamp or a clothespin. Finish the same way at the opposite end.

Ribbons come in a fabulous array of colors and textures ranging from vibrant jewel-colored velvets to soft, muted chiffons. They are available in many widths; narrow ribbons give the best coverage when wrapping; wider variations make superb rosettes and roses. Braiding and weaving different colored ribbons together can produce wonderful effects. Add coordinating jewel stones, pretty pearl beads, or even charms from a broken necklace for a touch of glamour.

Like ribbons, *braids* for dressmaking or for trimming home furnishings are available in richly textured finishes ideal for decorating barrettes and other hair accessories. They are wider than ribbons and are often more ornate; they don't need to cover a headband completely—add silk flowers, dazzling jewels, or ribbon roses between the braid to provide the perfect finishing touch. Wider braids can be stitched to padded headbands. Try highlighting decorative detail or pattern with

coordinating embroidery beads. Glue braids across the top of a simple hair comb rather than wrapping it, then decorate with jewels, beads, or pretty tassels for a more exotic finish.

Embroidery threads in cotton or silk, available in almost every color imaginable, look wonderful bound tightly around a plain headband or comb. Use them to create fun striped effects by carefully placing the colored threads side-by-side, or experiment with braiding, knotting, and weaving techniques for more unusual finishes. Colorful cords, leather thongs, and even fancy knitting yarns can also be used in the same way.

CREATING A DESIGN

Finding Inspiration

THE STARTING POINT IN ANY DESIGN IS FINDING INSPIRATION.
Ideas for jewelry designs can come from a visit to a museum or a library. Look to the ancient Egyptian, Roman, and Celtic civilizations, as well as the more recent Arts and Crafts and Art Deco periods, for ideas. A walk in the country or along the seashore can put you in touch with one of the greatest and most economical design source libraries: Mother Nature. Flowers and foliage, rocks and minerals, insect and animal life all can spur the imagination. The sky provides us with the sun, moon, and star motifs that are perfect for interpreting into jewelry forms. The sea washes up shells on the beach and sculpts pebbles and wood into interesting shapes.

Don't forget the materials you have on hand. Beads and fabrics can fall accidentally and often haphazardly together to create striking and unusual combinations. Paints and decorative finishes are fun to experiment with. Clays can be molded into unusual shapes and given textured finishes.

Working Out a Design

Once you have found your inspiration, try to sketch out different ideas on paper. You will need a sketch book, tracing paper, pencils, colored crayons, felt-tip markers (including gold and silver markers), an eraser, and a pencil sharpener. You don't have to draw works of art; rough sketches will suffice.

Work out the shape and size of the barrette and position any extra details like charm drops, beads, ribbons, or jewel stone decorations. It is important to keep symmetry and balance so that no one side appears strikingly different or out of proportion with the rest of the design. If you want to try any unusual decorative effects or hand paint intricate designs, begin on paper before moving on to the real thing.

copper hearts
tortoiseshell effect band

Papier Maché covered band decorated with bright spots

Decorate with small jewels

Fimo base shape painted gold + silver

Silk flowers or clay shapes to decorate hair comb or barrette

Clips & COMBS

For centuries, women have been using ornamental decorations to secure their hair in the latest style. Two of the most popular and practical designs today are the clip-fastening slide and the basic comb, which come in a wide variety of forms and can be used to hold anything from a ponytail to a chignon in place.

Clips and combs can be as simple or as ornate as you choose and are one of the simplest pieces of jewelry to make. You can buy metal clip-fastening bases from craft stores to make your own unique designs from papier-mâché or polymer clays or, alternatively, dress up plain plastic combs and slides with jewel stones, satin ribbons, or pretty silk flowers. Dazzling cut-glass stones set in mounts look sensational simply glued to plain metal clip bases, or you can create more interesting effects by anchoring strings of pretty beads to preformed holes in the base—twist, weave, or braid several strings together to achieve really dramatic finishes. Today's realistic-looking silk flowers are ideal for turning a simple clip or comb into something more special.

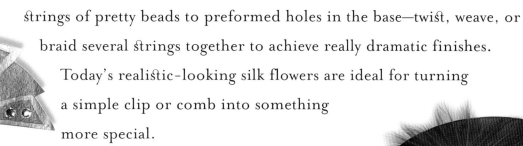

All the designs that follow are very versatile; once you have mastered the techniques shown, you might be inspired to interpret the basic idea in different ways. By adjusting the shape, color combinations, and decorative details, you can create many different effects.

Dazzling glass stones produce the best faux jewel effects. They can be found in a wide variety of shapes, including hearts and flowers.

Less-expensive acrylic and plastic jewel stones are also available in a fabulous range of colors and shapes.

Use the preformed holes on basic barrette clips to attach ornately beaded strings and try braiding, weaving, and twisting several together to create different effects.

Look for striking beads to use to decorate plain barrette clips—beads with flat surfaces can be glued directly to the clip's metal base, but round beads need to be wired or strung onto thread.

Dazzling
DIAMONDS

ACCORDING TO THE OLD SONG, DIAMONDS ARE A girl's best friend, and if you can't afford the real thing, sparkling cut glass has the same dazzling effect from a distance. The faceted jewel stones used to make this project come in faux emerald, sapphire, and a multitude of other precious jewel finishes. The settings can be bought with holes ready for sewing and threading, or plain for soldering, and both can be glued to basic barrettes to make unique, expensive-looking hair accessories. The basic idea invites experimentation; a collection of beautiful ceramic beads in patterns inspired by ancient Far Eastern dynasties looks superb simply glued in place. For another sparkling alternative, anchor strings of boldly colored glass rocailles to preformed holes in metal slide bases and braid, weave, or twist them to create different effects.

You Will Need

Cardboard
Epoxy adhesive
Spatula
Tweezers
Faceted jewel stones and matching mounts
Barrette base
Needle-nosed pliers

Getting Started

Look for a base that suits the thickness of your hair and that holds your hair in place for your chosen style. Measure the length of the base to gauge how many jewels you will need.

DAZZLING DIAMONDS

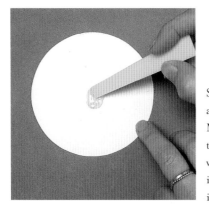

1.

Squeeze the epoxy onto a piece of cardboard. Mix the two elements together thoroughly with a spatula, following the package instructions.

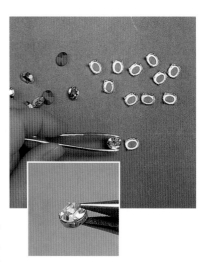

2.

Using tweezers, carefully place each stone in a mount and make sure it is level. Use the tips of a pair of needle-nosed pliers to fold the claws of the mount over the stones to secure them.

3.

Make sure the metal barrette is clean and grease-free before applying a layer of epoxy.

4.

Dab a small amount of epoxy onto the back of each mount and place it on the clip. Add as many stones as needed to completely cover the barrette base.

Variations on a Theme

BLUE NOTES BARRETTE

Cut three lengths of tiger tail. Slip one end of each through the hole at one end of the clip and secure with a calotte crimp—this gives a neater finish than knots.

Thread beads on each of the outside threads and attach to the opposite end of the barrette with a calotte crimp as in step 1. Bead the middle thread and work it over and under the others to create a woven effect.

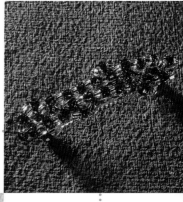

Just a few special beads mimicking classic china designs look sensational when glued in place. Create designs using the same type of beads, or mix coordinating colors and vary the way they are placed to achieve more original effects (right).

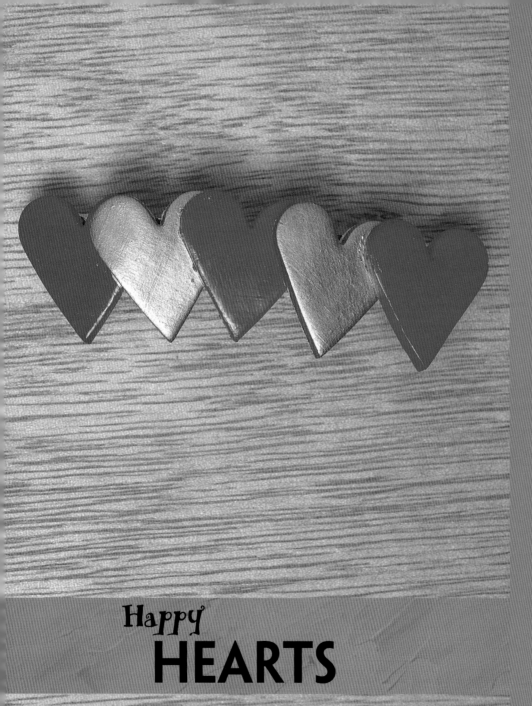

HAPPY
HEARTS

Design Tips

Sketch out design ideas on paper and work out the scale and balance of the idea before beginning the real thing.

Bake the shape on the clip base to ensure it sets in a curve; then secure with glue.

Smooth any rough edges with an emery board for a perfect finish.

Experiment with different paint effects and a variety of cookie cutters. A kitchen supply store can provide a wealth of inspiration with a wide variety of molds and cookie cutters in all kinds of designs.

Tiny flat-backed jewel stones glued to the clay shapes add extra glamour for evening styles.

THE SIMPLEST DESIGN IDEAS ARE OFTEN THE MOST effective, and this pretty barrette is a perfect example of what can be achieved using basic craft materials and elemental shapes. For this project, a heart-shaped cookie cutter is used to cut out motifs from polymer clay. The hearts are placed on a plain barrette clip, overlapping each other slightly, and then fired in a low-temperature oven. Polymer clay is one of the most versatile materials you can have in your supply box—it is easy to mold, sculpt, and cut into shape, and it comes in a wide range of colors. The different colors can be used on their own, blended together to produce a new color, or, with a little practice, mixed to achieve dramatic marbled effects.

Getting Started

Knead the polymer clay with your thumbs and fingers until it is really soft and pliable. This makes it much easier to roll and prevents cracking.

You Will Need

Polymer clay
in a neutral color
Rolling pin
Heart-shaped cookie cutter
Barrette base
Red and gold Plaka paint
Paintbrush
Varnish
All-purpose, clear-drying glue

HAPPY HEARTS

Knead the polymer clay thoroughly to soften and then roll out to a depth of ¼ inch / 0.6 cm. Using a heart-shaped cookie cutter, cut out as many shapes as you need to cover the clip base.

Place the hearts on the base, overlapping their edges slightly. Press the overlapped edges gently with your fingers (as you would with cookie dough) to ensure that they stick together. Bake the clay on the base in a low-temperature oven following the package instructions.

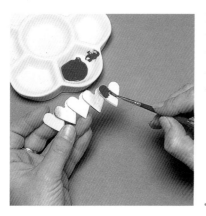

Carefully paint the hearts, leaving each one to dry before moving on to the next. Finish with a coat of varnish to give a glossy sheen.

Make sure the metal barrette is clean and grease-free before applying a layer of glue; then press the hearts in place and let dry.

Variations on a Theme

MARBLED STARS

1. Roll out two logs of polymer clay, each about the width of a pencil—one in white and another in red. Twist the logs around one another.

2. Roll the two logs together between the palms of your hands into a single, thicker log. Fold in half, twist together, and roll into a log again. Continue working in this way until you have the desired effect, taking care not to allow the colors to merge together into a single color.

3. Cut slices from the log and roll them out lightly. Then use tiny cookie cutters to make star shapes. Bake these on the clip base in a low-temperature oven. When cool, glue in place and varnish to finish.

This pretty daisy hair clip was painted with cold ceramic paints, which make it look as though it were made from delicate china (right).

Romantic
RIBBONS

Design Tips

Keep a scrap bag of ribbon and threads left over from other projects—they are perfect for decorating objects like hair combs.

Experiment with narrow strips of fabric as well as ribbons and threads—strips of denim or chambray can be used to create a sportier look for everyday wear.

Natural or dyed raffia is an excellent alternative to ribbons or cords.

The width of your ribbon will determine the size of a finished rosette—the wider the ribbon, the larger the rosette.

Stitch rosettes of different sizes together and finish with a central bead to create a pretty ribbon "flower."

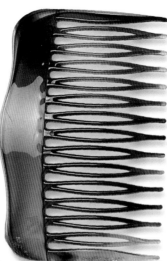

BASIC HAIR COMBS PROVIDE THE IDEAL BASE FOR creating pretty hair accessories because they can be dressed up with a wonderful variety of materials. Narrow ribbons, colorful silk embroidery threads, or fine satin cords can all be used to transform a basic plastic comb into something exceptional, especially if decorated with pretty coordinating beads or jazzy jewel stones. Cords and threads can be twisted or braided to create different looks, and ribbons look wonderful gathered into tiny rosettes that can be strewn across the top of a comb. Richly colored velvet ribbons decorated with sparkling diamanté are a wonderful combination for evening wear, and softer-hued satin, chiffon, or organza ribbons teamed with lustrous pearls look sensational worn by a bride or her attendants.

You Will Need

All-purpose, clear-drying glue
Plain plastic hair comb
Narrow, double-sided satin ribbon
Clothespin
Scissors
10–15 rice pearls
Tweezers

Getting Started

The amount of ribbon required depends on its width and the depth of the top of the comb. To get an idea of approximately how much you need, wrap the comb with string and measure this length.

ROMANTIC RIBBONS

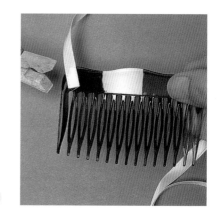

1. Dab a little glue on the right side of the comb, close to one end.

2. Place the end of the ribbon on the glue and hold it in place with a clothespin while it dries.

3. From the back, bring the ribbon through the gap between the first and second teeth of the comb. Take it over the top of the comb and back through the same gap, making sure you cover the starting point. Continue wrapping the ribbon through the gaps between each tooth of the comb twice, angling the ribbon carefully to make sure it covers the plastic top.

4. Before taking the ribbon through the last gap for the second time, dab a little glue close to the edge.

5.

Take the ribbon through to the back of the comb, trim, and secure with a dab of glue.

6.

To complete the comb, glue rice pearls to the ribbon, positioning them with tweezers to make sure they are evenly spaced.

Variations on a Theme

1.

Tiny rosettes of pastel and deep-pink ribbon look wonderful glued to cover the top of this simple comb. Cut two 2 ½-inch / 6.4-cm lengths of ribbon (¼ inch / 0.6 cm wide) in several shades of the same color. Join the short ends to form a circle and then run a gathering stitch along one long edge. Carefully pull this up and secure to form the rosettes. Glue in place on the top edge of a basic plastic hair comb.

Three rosettes made from the same ribbon are grouped together to create a stylish look (right).

Floral
FANTASY

Design Tips

Choose flowers carefully. You'll create a more authentic look by opting for varieties that are actually in season and that look the most genuine.

◎

Larger blooms look best on combs or slides that can be set to the side or back of the head rather than dead center on a headband.

◎

Newspaper and magazine reports of designer runway shows are a great source of inspiration for designs. Many top couturiers, especially the French, decorate models' hair with elegant or witty floral creations.

◎

Search out books that show you how to make your own silk flowers and have fun creating totally original designs.

◎

Simple designs create the most realistic effect, and a dab of scent helps complete the feel.

H AIR LOOKS AND FEELS WONDERFUL DRESSED WITH fresh flowers, but, sadly, this is not always practical—real flowers don't last long and are easily damaged. With care you can create a similar effect with today's fabulous array of silk flowers—the shapes and colors look so realistic that it is almost impossible to tell the difference from a distance. The most authentic-looking silk flowers are often the most expensive, but few are needed, so it is worth spending a little extra to achieve the right feel. Simply wire or glue dramatic single blooms or pretty sprays to combs, clips, or headbands to add the perfect finishing touch to a special outfit and add a spritz of eau de cologne to complete the effect.

You Will Need

Small silk flowers and pretty leaves
Scissors
Fine florist's or jeweler's wire
All-purpose, clear-drying glue
Tweezers
Plastic hair comb
Round-nosed pliers

Getting Started

Choose a hair comb with a patterned open-work top edge, like the one shown—these are much easier to wire flowers to. Make sure the wire is bound tightly around the flowers and the comb to secure them in place.

FLORAL FANTASY

1. Cut a selection of flowers in the main color, keeping each stalk as long as possible.

2. Select a single large leaf or several small leaves; then cut two or three fully open flowers plus one or two buds in the contrast color.

3. Using fine wire, bind three or four flowers in the main color tightly together in an attractive group.

4. Join this spray of flowers to the leaf in the same way.

5. Trim the stalks just below the base of one or two flowers in the main color and build a corsage effect by gluing them in place where required. Using tweezers, add a few buds in the contrast color in the same way.

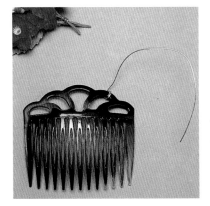

6. Wrap a length of wire tightly to the top edge of the comb approximately three-quarters of the way across.

7. Use the wire to bind the main corsage to the comb, wrapping it around the stems several times with pliers.

8. Wire together a smaller group of flowers in both the main and contrast colors; then carefully bind these to the comb to cover the spot where you joined the main corsage.

Variations on a Theme

A single bloom nestling on a bed of leaves completely disguises a very ordinary plastic hair clip (right).

A simple row of daisy heads, glued in place, transforms a functional hair comb into a desirable accessory in minutes (far right).

Fun FEATHERS

Design Tips

Feathers that are too long can be
carefully stripped back from the
base—never trim from the top or
you'll spoil the natural shape.

⊚

Look for unusual feathers—they can
even be from an unused feather duster
(see *Variations on a Theme*).

⊚

Feathers picked up on a walk or
in the garden need to be carefully
washed in a sterilizing solution
before you use them.

⊚

History books are a great source of
inspiration for design ideas.

⊚

Fishing tackle suppliers often
have a fascinating collection of
unusual feathers.

FEATHERS HAVE BEEN USED AS hair decorations by both men and women for hundreds of years and are back in vogue once again, having found favor with several top fashion designers. Single, elegant plumes look wonderful simply inserted into glamorous chignons or stitched to decorative headbands and worn "flapper" style. Smaller, more delicate varieties in dazzling hues can be glued to combs, clips, and slides. The choice of feathers varies from the striking natural plumes of peacock and pheasant to the fun and colorful marabou and ostrich, dyed in myriad colors to match any outfit. An extra dimension can be added with purchased or homemade coordinating beads.

You Will Need

Selection of small feathers
Large cabochon
Plain oval barrette
China marker
All-purpose, clear-drying glue
Toothpick

Getting Started

Trim the fine down at the base of each feather close to the quill before gluing in place to prevent the design from becoming too thick where all the feathers overlap.

FUN FEATHERS

1. Select the feathers you are going to use, placing large and small ones together in different groups. Use the larger ones for the sides of the design and the smaller ones for the top and bottom.

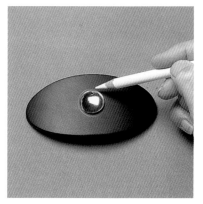

2. Place the cabochon in the center of the barrette and trace its circumference with a china marker.

3. Start at the three o'clock position on the china-graph circle and work back toward twelve o'clock. Glue larger feathers in place first; then graduate them slowly down in size toward the center top, making sure they curve in the same direction. Use a toothpick to position the feathers where you want them.

4. Glue the next quarter (three o'clock to six o'clock) in the same way, graduating the feathers down in size the closer you get to the bottom center point.

5. Work the other half of the slide in the same way, but choose feathers that curve in the opposite direction.

6. Fill in any gaps with appropriate-sized feathers and add a blob of glue to the center.

7. Position the cabochon over the central blob of glue and press firmly in place. Let dry completely.

Variations on a Theme

A spectacular peacock feather and ornate bronze beads combine to make a stunning hair clip (right).

These brightly colored plumes from a feather duster were used to make this jazzy hair clip. The addition of a glass jewel stone gives the design sophistication (far right).

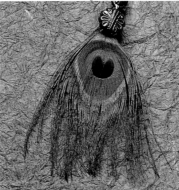

Creatively
COLORFUL

It is important to fire your design resting on the clip base to make sure it curves exactly to fit.

Sketch out design ideas on paper first. This helps to ensure that the scale is right and gives you a chance to experiment with different patterns and colors.

To get the best finish using polymer modeling clays, they should be kneaded well to soften and remove any air bubbles, which will create a smooth surface when the clay is rolled out.

Look through art history books or gallery catalogues for inspiration for both designs and use of color.

The elliptical shape used for this design is just one example of the many shapes you can use as a base. Experiment with different ideas, but bear in mind how and where you want to wear the clip and make sure it is the right size.

THIS BOLD, BRIGHT HAIR CLIP WITH ITS STRIKING geometric design was influenced by the inspired paintings of Dutch artist Piet Mondrian. The base and pattern were created using modern polymer clays. These clays provide a versatile modeling medium for craft jewelry designers and are available in a wide range of colors that can be used on their own, blended together to create marbled effects, or painted and textured to produce totally unique finishes. For this design, different colors were used to create a pattern on top of a plain clay base. You need only tiny amounts of clay for the lines, squares, and circles, so this is a great way to use up scraps left over from other projects.

You Will Need

Cardboard
Felt-tip pens
Scissors
Polymer clay in the base color
Small amounts of polymer clay
in 6 bright colors
Rolling pin
Craft knife
Modeling tools (optional)
Clip base
All-purpose, clear-drying glue
Varnish
Paintbrush

Getting Started

Leave the polymer clay wrapped in a plastic bag on top of a towel on a warm radiator to help speed up the softening time, especially for old clay. You can buy special preparations produced by the manufacturer that do the same job.

CREATIVELY COLORFUL

Carefully draw out your chosen base shape on cardboard and cut it out.

Draw your pattern on one side of the template using felt-tip pens to illustrate where the different colors are to be placed.

Knead the base-color polymer clay until it is soft; then roll it out to a depth of approximately ¼ inch / 0.6 cm. Using a craft knife, carefully cut around the cardboard template.

Use the pattern drawn on your template as a guide to create the design on top of the base shape. To make the lines, roll the clay into ¹/₁₆ inch / 1.5 mm logs and place on top of the base as required. Smooth gently and press in place using your fingers or the tip of a modeling tool. Complete the design with tiny squares, rectangles, and circles.

5.

To smooth the surface and ensure that the pattern stays in place, gently roll over it with a rolling pin.

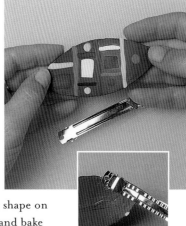

6.

Place the clay shape on the clip base and bake in a low-temperature oven following the package instructions. When cool, glue the clip to the clay and let dry completely.

7.

Finish with a coat of varnish to bring out the depth of the colors and add a glossy sheen.

Variations on a Theme

Tiny jewel stones add the perfect finishing touch to a simple yet stylish design in fashionable monochrome (right).

Another bold geometric pattern is worked in checkerboard effect. Choose colors to match a favorite outfit (far right).

Fan-
TASTIC

Design Tips

Sketch out design ideas on paper first and experiment with different patterns and use of colors. You can then trace your pattern lightly onto the clay after firing.

When you choose to paint the hardened clay, select a base color that is neutral. If you have an unsuitable color to use up, paint it first with a primer-like gesso.

A light-colored base will allow you to draw the outline of your design directly onto the clay before painting.

Make sure you rest the clay shape on the clip base when baking to ensure it curves exactly to fit the clip.

Polymer modeling clays should be kneaded well to soften and remove any air bubbles, creating a smooth surface when the clay is rolled out. If the clay still has bubbles or cracks, scoop it up and continue to knead before rolling out again.

THIS CHIC, FAN-SHAPED HAIR SLIDE WAS INSPIRED BY an exquisite brooch and earrings set seen in a jewelry design catalogue. The three-dimensional original was worked in precious metals and set with genuine diamonds. For this design, clever use of polymer clay, crystal jewel stones, and metallic paints created a similar effect for a fraction of the cost. The same base shape inspired the fun "deck-of-cards" design and the rainbow-hued fan shown in *Variations on a Theme.* By choosing to handpaint a plain polymer clay shape, you increase the number of design options infinitely. These can be ultra-simple and stylized like the ideas shown here, or, if you are a competent artist, the clay shapes can provide the perfect blank canvas for your artistic talents.

Getting Started

To achieve a perfect fan shape, first draw a semicircle to the size required on tracing paper. Using a compass or protractor, mark the curved edge at regular intervals. Mark the center on the straight edge and draw lines from this point out to join the marks on the curved edge. Mark ¼ inch / 0.6 cm from the curved edge on each radiating line and draw a line from this mark to the next point on the curved edge.

You Will Need

Cardboard
Pen
Ruler
Scissors
Block of polymer clay
in a neutral color
Rolling pin
Craft knife
Clip base
Pencil
All-purpose, clear-drying glue
Gold and silver metallic paints
Paintbrush
12 small flat-backed jewel stones
1 larger flat-backed jewel stone
Varnish

47

FAN-TASTIC

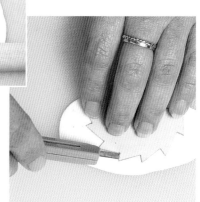

1. Carefully draw out the base shape on cardboard and cut it out.

2. Knead the polymer clay until it is soft; then roll it out to a depth of approximately ¼ inch / 0.6 cm. Lay the cardboard template on the clay and, using a craft knife, carefully cut out the shape.

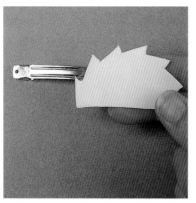

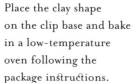

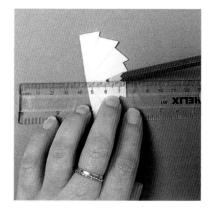

4. Using a pencil, lightly draw your design on the clay.

3. Place the clay shape on the clip base and bake in a low-temperature oven following the package instructions.

5. Turn the shape over and glue the clip base in place. Leave until completely dry.

6. Carefully paint the design on the clay. Paint one section at a time and let dry before moving on to the next. Remember to paint all the edges and the reverse side.

7. Glue the jewel stones in place, using tweezers to position them accurately. Apply only a small amount of glue because too much can spoil the finished effect. A final coat of varnish will protect the paint finish.

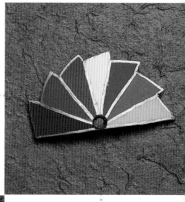

Variations on a Theme

A hand of playing cards inspired this variation. Draw simple shapes directly on the clay and paint the details with a fine brush (right).

Brilliant primary colors outlined with a gold marker pen and finished with a dazzling jewel stone creates a more electric variation on the same theme (far right).

Use torn strips of newspaper—
the rough edges produce less
obvious joints.

Carefully overlap each piece and
smooth the edges with your fingers
to release any trapped air or
lumpy paste.

Using two different-colored
newspapers makes it easier to
distinguish between the layers.

You can use wallpaper paste or PVA
glue as an adhesive. Wallpaper paste
is easier to deal with because it's less
tacky than PVA, but PVA produces a
stronger finish. Mix the two together
to a consistency of thick cream or use
PVA for the last few layers.

All the layers can be applied at once,
but the smoothest finish is achieved
by allowing each one to dry before
applying the next.

All
SQUARE

PAPIER-MÂCHÉ IS ONE OF THE MOST INEXPENSIVE AND fun ways of making jewelry. Once you get hooked on this hobby, you will never cease to be amazed at the sheer variety of designs that can be made from just an old newspaper and a bit of wallpaper paste. To make this wonderfully ornate hair slide, the basic layering technique was used to cover and stiffen a simple cardboard base. The decorative detail was added later with ordinary household plaster filler that was applied using an icing bag joined to a tip with a small hole. The finished result is a wearable work of art and just one example of how versatile papier-mâché is for the craft jeweler. Both *Variations on a Theme* are based on the same simple square shapes and illustrate how totally different effects can be achieved by using different materials.

You Will Need

Cardboard
Pencil
Ruler
Craft knife
Scissors
Icing bag
PVA glue (optional)
Wallpaper paste
Plaster filling
Newspaper torn into small strips
Clip base
Artist's gesso
Emery board
Gold spray paint
Red acrylic paint
Fine paintbrush
All-purpose, clear-drying glue
2 large and 1 small
flat-backed jewel stones

Getting Started

Mix up a small amount of wallpaper paste following instructions on the package. Cover the paste with plastic wrap or store in a lidded container until you need it.

ALL SQUARE

From the cardboard, cut out 2 squares, ¾" x ¾" (2 cm x 2 cm), 1 square, 1¼" x 1¼" (3 cm x 3 cm), and 1 strip, 1¼" x 2¾" (1 cm x 7 cm). Coat one side of the strip with PVA glue and stick on the squares centrally, in the order shown.

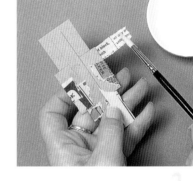

Add wallpaper paste to the strips of newspaper and cover the cardboard shape for a first layer, smoothing the paper flat with your fingers.

Replace the central bar in the clip and then paint the base with artist's gesso—this acts as an undercoat and prevents the newsprint from showing through the painted finish.

Before adding the next layer, open the clip base and remove the central bar. Lay the clip, as shown, along the center of the narrow strip of cardboard. Continue adding even layers of pasted paper over the entire shape, covering the clip base and curving the cardboard to fit at the same time. Let it dry completely after every third layer of paper has been added. You will need to use 6 to 8 layers in all.

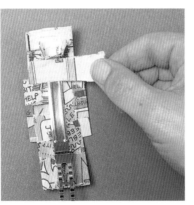

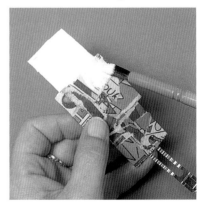

Using a faint pencil, lightly draw the outline of the design you want to work in plaster filler directly onto the base.

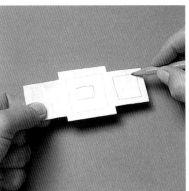

Squeeze the plaster filler into an icing bag topped with a fine tip and squeeze it gently, following the marked lines of your pattern. Leave to harden. Use the rougher side of an emery board to smooth and shape the edges of the raised design until you are satisfied with the finished effect.

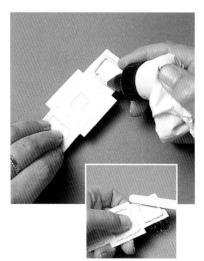

Spray the shape evenly with gold paint. When dry, add decorative detail using red acrylic paint and finish with coordinating jewel stones glued in place with a clear-drying adhesive.

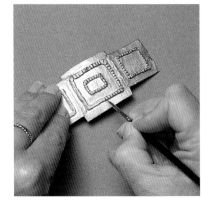

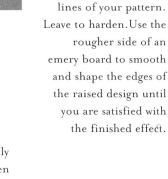

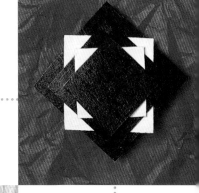

Variations on a Theme

Turned on their side to form diamonds and worked in glittering crystal and jet-black beads, the cardboard squares take on a completely different look (right).

For this striking design, a thicker cardboard was used, and, instead of using papier-mâché techniques, each square was given a coat of PVA glue after painting (far right)

Beautiful BANDS

Bands in one form or another have been used to decorate and hold hair in place since the beginning of time, and the styles have varied from simple ribbons to ornate jewel-encrusted circlets and tiaras. A famous fresco from the Royal Palace at Knossos shows ladies of the Minoan court wearing ribbons just above their foreheads and tied at the nape of the neck; the rest of their hair is threaded with chains of precious jewels. Books on the history of fashion—and hairstyles in particular—illustrate wonderful examples like this and are a great source of inspiration for design ideas.

The headband has recently become fashionable again, and a simple plastic or fabric-covered headband provides the perfect base for all kinds of decorative finishes. They can be as modest or as fancy as you choose, to suit your own personal style or a particular special occasion. You can create all kinds of different effects with the amazing variety of materials available, including luxurious braids and dazzling faux jewels. Plain white plastic bases are available from craft suppliers, but you can also use the ideas shown here to dress up an inexpensive band bought at a local drugstore.

When working out your design, it is important to create an overall balanced effect. Position motifs and any decorative detail with care so that they form a regular pattern and keep their sizes in proportion.

Hot
SPOTS

NEOPRENE IS A FASCINATING ADDITION TO THE WIDE range of craft materials currently available. It has a wonderfully tactile finish that is like soft rubber and is extremely versatile. Use it to create flat motifs or three-dimensional shapes—it can even be used to make chunky rolled beads in the same way as you would with paper. Available from craft stores in sheet form or precut shapes like flowers, hearts, and circles, neoprene comes in a wide range of colors. You can draw shapes on it easily and cut intricate details with scissors or a craft knife. For this fun design, a single-hole punch was used to make tiny circles, which were then glued to a painted plastic headband in a five-dice pattern. A craft pack of circles in bright assorted colors is perfect for this design, because buying individual sheets in all the colors would be wasteful unless you have other projects in mind.

Getting Started

The five-dice pattern used for this project gives a polka-dot effect but keeps the overall design regular and symmetrical. By working with six colors, each pattern will be different.

Plastic headband
Emery board
Black acrylic paint
Paintbrush
Neoprene in 6 different colors
Single-hole punch
Tweezers
All-purpose, clear-drying glue

HOT SPOTS

1. Scuff the surface of the band lightly with an emery board to provide a surface that the paint can adhere to. Don't be too rough or else scratches will show through the paint.

2. Paint the band completely and let it dry balanced on the edge of a jar.

3. Use the hole punch to cut tiny circles in different colors from the neoprene—the number required will depend on how you space them.

4. Using tweezers, position the circles on the painted band, alternating the colors and working in a pattern like the five on a pair of dice, and glue them in place.

Variations on a Theme

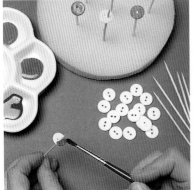

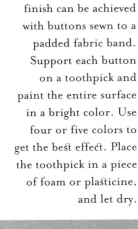

1. A more dramatic finish can be achieved with buttons sewn to a padded fabric band. Support each button on a toothpick and paint the entire surface in a bright color. Use four or five colors to get the best effect. Place the toothpick in a piece of foam or plasticine, and let dry.

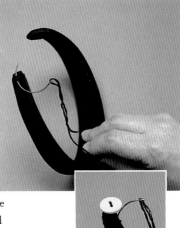

2. Using six strands of embroidery cotton, tie a knot in one end and make a small stitch on the right side of the band close to one end. Sew on the first button, positioning it so that it covers the starter knot. Bring the needle out where the next button is to be placed—they should be evenly spaced along the band.

3. Sew on the last button, work a couple of tiny oversew stitches under, and insert the needle back into the fabric toward the center of the band, bringing it out on a side edge as far up as you can. Pull the thread taut and cut—the tail end should disappear inside the band.

Glue flat-backed crystal stones to a thin headband for a sparkling hair accessory to wear on special occasions (right).

Beautiful BRAIDS

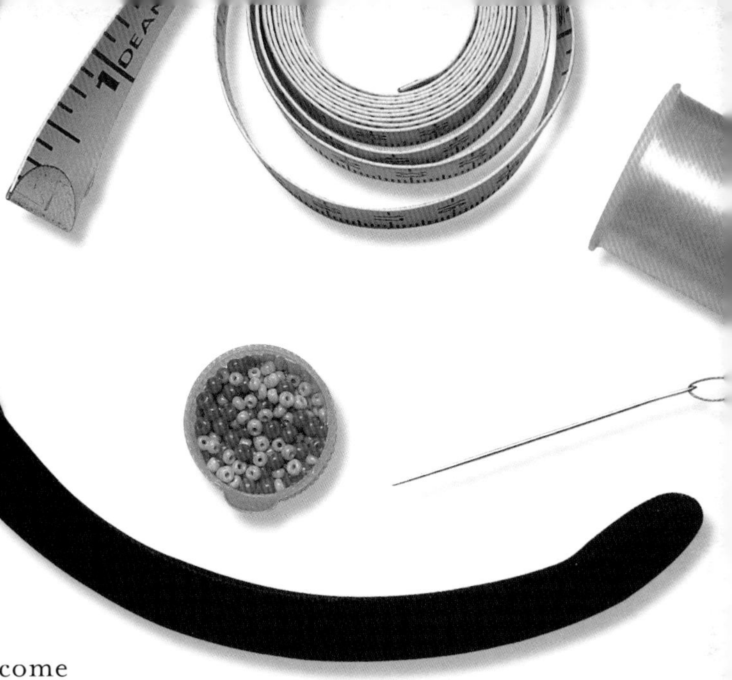

W ITH A PIECE OF BRAID, a selection of beads in several shades of the same color, and a little imagination, you can transform a basic fabric band into a striking hair decoration. Braids available for dressmaking and home furnishing can be used for the ideas shown here. They can be plain, or patterned in smooth or textured finishes, and come in every color imaginable. For this project, a colorful braid was carefully beaded in coordinating colors to highlight the bold pattern and sewn with invisible thread to a plain padded band. The sparkling sequined variation was bought already beaded and is perfect for special evenings. A silky textured braid wrapped around a plain band and finished with ribbon roses could be worn by a bridesmaid for a summer wedding.

You Will Need

Padded fabric hair band
Tape measure
Length of braid (about 18 inches /
45.7 cm, depending on the band)
All-purpose, clear-drying glue
Selection of coordinating
embroidery beads
Beading needle
Thread in several shades
of the same color
Invisible thread
Scissors

Getting Started

To determine the amount of beads you will use when decorating your own braid, count the number of beads used in one inch of braid and multiply by the length of the band.

BEAUTIFUL BRAIDS

Measure the band and add 1 inch / 2.5 cm to allow for two ½-inch / 1.3-cm hems.

Cut the braid to the correct length.

Turn ½ inch / 1.3 cm to the wrong side at each end and glue in place or hem with invisible thread.

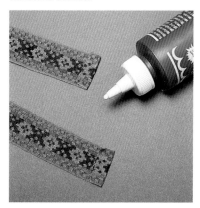

Using the braid's pattern as a guide, work out where you are going to stitch the beads. For this design, beads in the two main colors of the braid were used to highlight the geometric pattern.

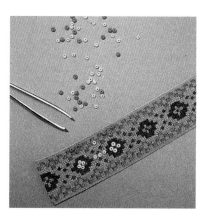

5. Sew one color in place first, working clusters on the same length of thread and single beads individually. Use a tiny backstitch under each bead to hold them in position securely.

6. Sew the second colored beads in place in the same way as the first.

7. Oversew the braid to the band using invisible thread, taking care to keep the tension even.

Variations on a Theme

Glittering gold sequined braid was glued directly to a plain band to make this glamorous evening hair decoration (right).

Textured silky braid and pretty ribbon roses combine to make a headband that is perfect for summer weddings (far right).

Evening
STARS

Design Tips

Plan your design carefully before starting on the real thing. Measure the band and draw it out on paper; then experiment with arrangements of beads and jewel stones.

Look for shaped jewel stones, such as hearts, stars, and flowers, to use as central focal points or as part of the overall pattern.

Use jewel stones with preformed holes that you can sew directly onto fabric-covered bands. To attach them, use invisible thread for a sophisticated finish or matching, jewel-colored embroidery threads for colorful accents.

Experiment with different combinations of sophisticated crystals and pearls to make brilliant, bold patterns.

Look for bands in interesting fabrics like velvet, satin, and jacquard or cover your own basic bands.

COMBINE DAZZLING JEWEL STONES WITH GLITTERING glass bugle beads for the ultimate hair accessory for special evenings. Faceted flat-backed jewels come in a wonderful range of sizes, colors, and shapes to add a touch of sparkle to different jewelry projects.

The jewels can be made from acrylic, plastic, or glass; acrylic shapes are the least expensive but can react with some adhesives, which spoils the finished effect. Glass and plastic jewels are available plain or with custom-made holes for sewing in place; the style you select depends upon your chosen design. Bugle beads are usually made of glass and come in bright jewel tones of varying lengths. For this design, they radiate out from the jeweled star shapes and also form part of the pattern between the main motifs.

Getting Started

Select flat-backed jewel stones and bugle beads in colors that work well together and in sizes suitable for the width of the band. Make sure all surfaces to be glued are free of dust and grease to ensure the best contact.

You Will Need

Fabric-covered headband
Tape measure
Paper
Pencil
Tailor's chalk
Tweezers
All-purpose, clear-drying glue
Flat-backed jewel stones
Coordinating bugle beads

EVENING STARS

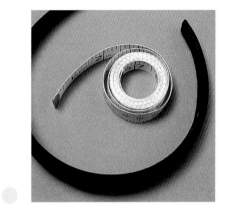

1. Measure the length of the band.

3. Measure and mark the position of each motif with a tailor's chalk dot on the actual band.

2. Work out the positioning of your motifs and draw them out on paper. Start at the center point and work outward, making sure the design is the same on each side and positioned symmetrically.

4. Using tweezers, glue the jewel stones for the center motif in position first and let dry, resting the band on a jar or mug.

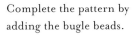

5. Glue the rest of the main jewel stones in place and let dry.

6. Complete the pattern by adding the bugle beads.

Variations on a Theme

Give a plain plastic headband a new lease on life by decorating it with dazzling faceted jewels. Space the stones out evenly along the length of the band and place larger stones toward the center to create the right balance (right).

These striking gilt shells were found in the bottom of a rummage box at a local bead store and cost next to nothing. They look stunning glued to form bold motifs on a plain headband, with pretty jewel stones adding a touch a glamour (far right).

Magical
METALWORK

If you can't find sheet metal, use the preformed metal shapes available for enameled jewelry designs.

Experiment with different shaped motifs and textured finishes, using a variety of objects.

With soft metals you can turn under the edges just like fabric to make them smooth, or file them with a fine metal hand file.

Treat the metal like fabric, clipping into curves and corners to turn under the edges of more intricate shapes.

You can produce totally different effects using enamel paints to color the metal and highlight the textured finish.

Experiment with relief designs, using a knitting needle or substantial sewing needle to work the designs.

WORKING WITH METAL IS MUCH EASIER THAN YOU'D imagine, and it opens up a new world of design opportunities. You don't need much in the way of special tools or skills to create striking motifs to decorate simple headbands and make them look really special. Soft sheet metals like tin, copper, and pewter are easy to cut and shape using heavy-duty scissors, tin cutters, or a basic craft knife, and the edges can be smoothed with a fine metal hand file. Sheet metal is available from craft or sculptor's suppliers, usually in rolls of set length. Depending on its thickness, it can be given an attractive textured finish by hammering it with the end of a paintbrush, dragging a metal comb over it, or just beating it with a small hammer. Cut the metal into small shapes and glue them to a basic band, spaced at regular intervals.

You Will Need

Basic headband
Tape measure
China marker
Emery board
Small sheet of sheet copper
(a 2-inch / 5.1-cm square)
Paintbrush or small hammer
Steel ruler
Tin cutters
All-purpose, clear-drying glue
Charm

Getting Started

It is a good idea to test-hammer the metal before starting the project. This will help you judge how much pressure you need to use and how to position the end of the paintbrush to get an even pattern over the surface.

MAGICAL METALWORK

Measure the length of
the band.

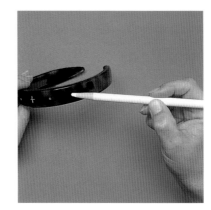

Work out your design
and mark the position
of the center motif
on the band with the
china marker. Position
the rest of the motifs in
the same way, working
out from the center
and keeping the design
symmetrical.

Scuff the plastic band with
an emery board where
each motif is to be set to
provide a surface that the
glue can adhere to.

Lay the copper on a soft
surface—a rubber cutting
mat is ideal, but a pile
of newspapers will work
as well. Hammer the
surface with the end of
the paintbrush.

5.

Using a china marker and a ruler, divide the shape into ⅜-inch / 1-cm squares.

6.

Carefully cut out the squares using tin cutters or heavy-duty household scissors.

7.

Rotate the squares to form diamonds and glue in position. Glue a charm to the central motif to add a special finish.

Variations on a Theme

Narrow strips of copper were wrapped tightly around a velvet band to make it look more ornate. Glue the ends on the inside with all-purpose glue (right).

Patterned flat beads were used on this fabric band to achieve a similar effect. Glue the beads in clusters or space at regular intervals to create different finishes (far right).

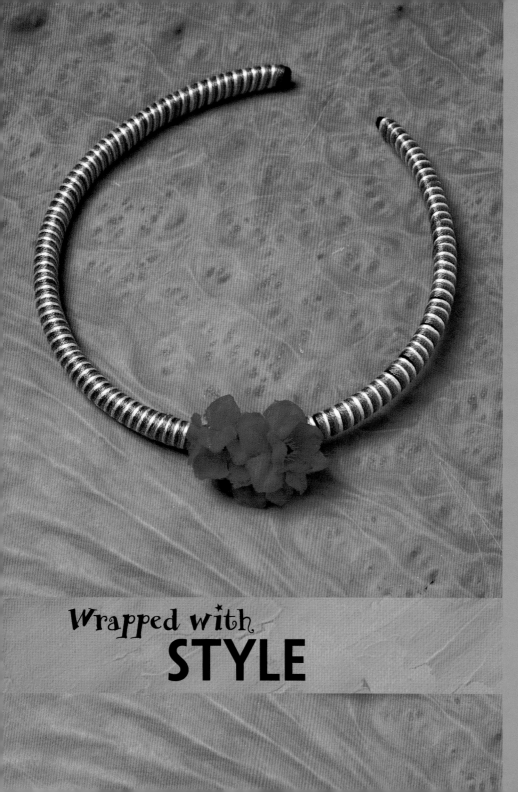

Wrapped with
STYLE

Use embroidery threads left over from other projects and join colors on the inside, unseen side of the band. The raw ends can then be covered with a length of binding or ribbon glued in place.

You need only small amounts of fabric to cover a band and can find wonderful bargains in remnant boxes. Look for special fabrics that are expensive to buy on a roll.

Plan your design before working on the real thing—experiment with different ideas and materials. Use double-sided adhesive tape to secure in position temporarily to get an idea of the finished look.

Keep charms from broken pieces of jewelry to recycle and use to add a decorative highlight to a fabric or thread-covered band.

Silk flowers, ribbon roses, and bows can all be used to add a perfect finishing touch to designs. They can be bought ready-made or handmade, if you have the time.

A SIMPLE PLASTIC HEADBAND PROVIDES THE PERFECT foil for creative decoration and can be bought at little cost from department stores, drugstores, and craft stores. They can be decorated simply by gluing attractive beads, jewels, and shells in position or given a fancier finish by covering them completely with colorful threads or glamorous fabrics. Wrapping basic bands with strands of embroidery cottons or silks is an easy way to make a hair accessory to coordinate with a favorite outfit and takes no time at all. You can also use a variety of other materials in the same way, including pretty braids, cords, ribbons, raffia, and even decorative papers. Add a flamboyant finish with a spray of silk flowers, an ornate charm, or rich bead embroidery.

You Will Need

Basic plastic headband
Emery board
Skeins of embroidery threads
in different colors
Scissors
All-purpose, clear-drying glue
Clamp
Coordinating silk flowers

Getting Started

Measure the length of the band. Quickly wrap about one-fourth of the band, measure this length and multiply it by 4 to give you the approximate amount of thread required—remember to add a little extra for the ends.

WRAPPED WITH STYLE

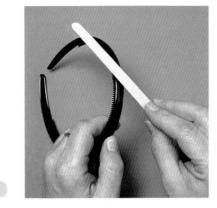

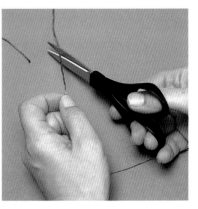

1. Scuff the plastic band with an emery board to provide a surface for the glue to adhere to and stop the threads from sliding around.

2. Following the directions in *Getting Started,* cut threads to length. Three colors in the same shade were used to make this design.

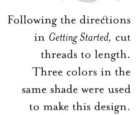

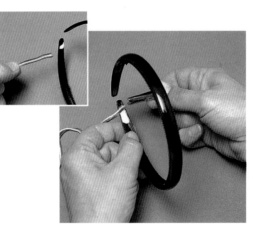

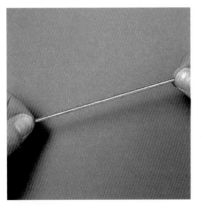

3. Smooth the threads out so that they lie side by side.

4. Dab a small amount of glue on the inside edge of the band and place the group of threads on top. Use a clamp to hold the threads in position while the glue sets.

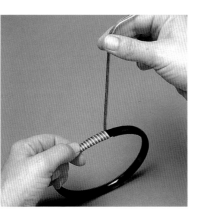

Wrap the threads
tightly and evenly
around the band,
adding an occasional
blob of glue to hold
them in place.

6.

Trim the spray of
flowers, cutting each
stalk as closely as
possible to the bloom.

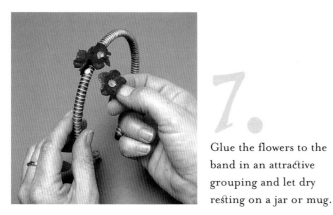

7.

Glue the flowers to the
band in an attractive
grouping and let dry
resting on a jar or mug.

Variations on a Theme

Pleated organza and the charm from a broken earring decorate this plain padded
fabric band. Sew a strip of fabric into a tube two to three times longer than the
band and wide enough to cover the broadest section of the band (right).

Pretty braid and bold silk flowers were used to transform a basic band into a
stunning bridal accessory (far right).

Hair
SLIDES

The idea of securing hair in place with a simple pin was originally used by the ancient civilizations of Egypt, Greece, and Rome, thousands of years before clip-fastening mechanisms had been invented. Today's designs use the pin to secure both the hair and a decorative base in place and are one of the easiest styles of hair ornaments to make.

Hair slides can be any style, from chic to fun and funky. The pins are easy to make from wooden skewers, which can be cut to size and decorated in a variety of ways—paint them to match the base or wrap them with satin ribbons and fine fancy cords. Look for unusual ideas like a children's plastic embroidery needle or the cable needles used to create intricate textured knitting designs. The bases can be fashioned from an infinite variety of materials including cardboard, polymer clay, fabric, and even papier-mâché.

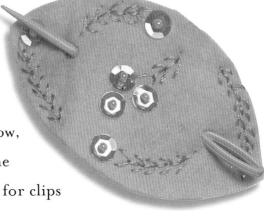

Once you have mastered the techniques that follow, you can create your own variations inspired by the same themes. You can also use some of the ideas for clips shown in the first section and position the holes to take the pin, where required.

Shining
STAR

Design Tips

Position the holes for the pin and curve rigid bases so that they sit neatly on your chosen hair style—the curve needed to secure a ponytail is greater than that required to hold your hair in a chignon. Use a store-bought design that fits the required style as a guide, or wrap plasticine or air-dry clay in plastic (so it won't get in your hair) and use it to make a template.

❁

A useful source for basic motifs are catalogues illustrating stamps and stencils; for more elaborate designs, look at history books and the patterns used by ancient civilizations.

❁

Draw your design onto tracing paper and transfer it to the metal by following the outline with a darning needle, making light indentations where you intend to position the holes, or work the design freehand using a china marker.

❁

Use tin cutters to cut out thicker metals and wear protective gloves and glasses.

THE INSPIRATION FOR THE PIERCED design of this hair slide comes from traditional punched tin work popular with the Shaker movement. It not only is easy to master, but also provides scope for creating a wide variety of different motifs once you gain a little experience and get used to the feel of the metal. Spectacular relief designs can also be worked on the metal simply by using the tip of a knitting needle over a traced design. Once you have mastered the basic punched-tin techniques you can experiment with more elaborate designs. For example, stars, moons, hearts, flowers, stylized animals, or insects are easy shapes to cut from the sheet metal. Embellish them with either pierced or etched patterns to make original hair slides or clip-fastening barrettes.

You Will Need

Tracing paper
Thick cardboard
Steel ruler
Craft knife
Sheet metal
Darning needle
PVA glue
Scissors or tin cutters
Single-hole punch
Panel pin
Small tin hammer
All-purpose, clear-drying glue
Wooden skewer
Silver paint
Paintbrush

Getting Started

You will need a piece of sheet metal approximately 8 inches x 5 inches / 20.3 cm x 12.7 cm. Draw out the shape on paper first and place tracing paper over it. With a pencil, transfer the motif onto the tracing paper in dot form. Space the dots evenly and make sure the design fits centrally on the barrette.

SHINING STAR

Cut out an oblong of cardboard 3½ inches / 8.9 cm x 1½ inches / 3.8 cm using a craft knife for smooth, even edges.

Center the cardboard on the piece of metal, leaving a ⅜-inch / 1-cm border on all edges. Use the tip of a darning needle to draw around the cardboard, impressing the shape in the metal. Paint both sides of the cardboard mount with PVA glue to give it flexibility. Cut out another piece of metal to the exact size of the cardboard to use as a backing.

Use scissors or tin cutters to cut across each corner at a 45° angle. Place the PVA-coated cardboard mount back on the piece of metal and fold over all four edges along the indented lines.

Measure and mark the positions for the holes to hold the barrette pin on the cardboard-mounted main piece and the backing—these should be ¼ inch / 0.6 cm in from the edge and positioned centrally across the width. Punch out holes using a hole punch.

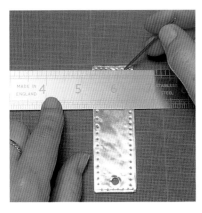

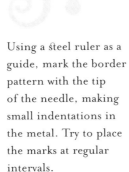

5.

Using a steel ruler as a guide, mark the border pattern with the tip of the needle, making small indentations in the metal. Try to place the marks at regular intervals.

6.

Position the tracing of the motif centrally on the metal and transfer by pressing the tip of the needle through each pencil dot. Place the shape on a suitable surface and gently hammer a panel pin through each indentation on both the border and the motif to give the design greater definition.

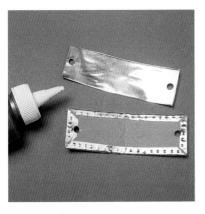

7.

Glue the backing in place using an all-purpose glue, taking care not to get any on the front of the barrette. Let dry. Trim a wooden skewer to size and paint it silver. Gently curve the barrette around a mug and insert the pin.

Variations on a Theme

This stunning copper design was inspired by the decoration on an ancient Celtic shield. The intricate pattern was traced onto the soft metal with a knitting needle (right).

The background of a Phoenician stone relief inspired this ornate pattern (far right), which was drawn on soft-sheet aluminum in the same way as the copper Celtic shield.

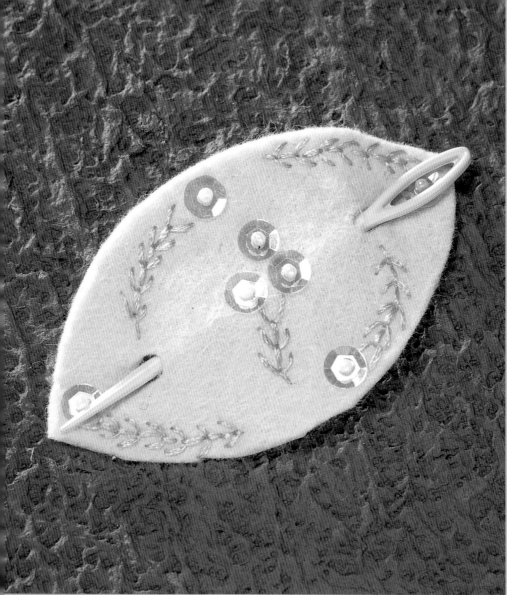

Enchanting
EMBROIDERED FELT

THE USE OF FABRIC IN jewelry design has added another dimension to the craft and opened up a whole new world of design ideas. If you can use a needle and thread, you can transform remnants of fabric, scraps of embroidery thread, and leftover beads into pretty barrettes. Simple embroidery stitches worked by hand or on the sewing machine add texture and detail to simple fabric shapes—choose several subtle shades of the same color for a dainty finish or bold, bright metallics for something more flamboyant. Complementary beads and sequins can be used as delicate highlights or in greater numbers to create a rich, ornate finished look. Transforming your finished design into a barrette is easy with the wide range of iron-on adhesives available—they fuse the fabric to cardboard, leather, and even wood.

You Will Need

Cardboard
Compass
Pencil
Scissors
Felt (a 5-inch / 12.7-cm square)
Piece of firm iron-on interfacing
Embroidery silk
Embroidery needle
Sequins
Tiny embroidery pearl beads
Single-hole punch
Plastic needle to fasten the barrette
Iron-on adhesive

Getting Started

To draw an oval, first draw a circle 2 inches / 5.1 cm in diameter. With the compass set to the same measurement, move the point to the edge of the circle and draw an arc, taking the pencil from edge to edge, passing across the center point of the drawn circle.

ENCHANTING EMBROIDERED FELT

1.

Draw an oval on the cardboard as described in *Getting Started* and cut it out. Place the interfacing on the felt and cut to size, then iron on following the instructions provided.

2.

Place the cardboard template on top of the interfacing, trace it in pencil, and cut it out.

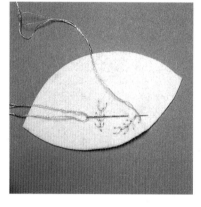

3.

Mark the position of your chosen motifs on the interfacing. Using two strands of silk, embroider the design— this design is worked in a pretty feather stitch.

4.

Add sequins as required. Working with a single strand of silk, bring the needle through the central hole of the sequin from the wrong side. Take the needle through a tiny pearl bead and back through the central hole of the sequin. Tie off on the wrong side.

5.

Measure and mark the positions for the barrette-pin holes and cut out using a hole punch. The holes should be placed in line with the points of the oval and approximately ¾ inch / 1.9 cm in from the edges, depending on the size of the fastening pin.

6.

Check the length of the fastening pin and set the holes appropriately so it sits centrally on the motif as shown.

7.

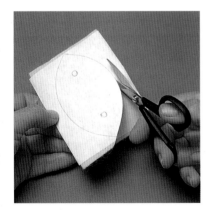

Cut another oval from the remaining felt and apply iron-on adhesive to one side following the instructions. Remove the paper backing and place the embroidered motif right-side down on top of a towel. Place the adhesive side of the second oval on top, matching edges exactly and press following the instructions provided.

Variations on a Theme

This safari design fabric was decorated with tiny beads and textured glitter paints. Back with suede or leather and punch out holes for the pin (right).

Embroider a paisley shape with tiny beads to highlight the colors and pattern and back with suede, leather, or felt. To make the pin, wrap a wooden skewer with twisted paper cord (far right).

Mock Croc
BARRETTE

Experiment with different motifs and sketch them out on paper first. Work out color combinations and position any design details before starting on the real thing.

Look for different objects to use as pins to fasten the barrette—plastic cable needles used for knitting, chopsticks, and colored crayons can all be used to add a fun finish.

Make sure the clay is rolled out to a reasonable thickness—if it is too thin it will snap when worn.

To add jewel stones and beads, press them into the clay to make an impression. Remove and bake as usual. When hard, add a little glue in the imprints and press the stones in place. Glass jewel stones and beads can be pressed into the clay and baked, but plastic will melt.

THIS FUN CROCODILE HAIR SLIDE is just one of many creations you can make using today's versatile polymer modeling clays. They come in a wide range of colors that can be used to make plain shapes, like the crocodile, or multicolored designs like the fish and butterfly variations. Once kneaded, the clay can be rolled out like just like pastry and cut using a cardboard template and craft knife or preformed cookie cutters. The surface is soft enough to add texture and design detail in other colors. The finished shape needs to sit on something curved as it is baked to create the right shape for a barrette, and you may need to experiment a little to get it just right.

You Will Need

Cardboard
Pencil
Scissors
Block of green polymer clay
Rolling pin
Craft knife
Wooden skewer or toothpick
Varnish
Paintbrush
Copper wire
Round-nosed pliers
Verdigris-copper beads
Flat-backed emerald crystals
All-purpose, clear-drying glue

Getting Started

To ensure that the hair slide will have a perfect fit, wrap a strip of plasticine approximately the same length and width as the finished design in clear plastic wrap and position it on your head. Insert a wooden skewer through both holes, then carefully remove it, keeping the shape. Use this as a pattern for the clay shape and bake the finished design over something oven-proof with a similar curve.

MOCK CROC BARRETTE

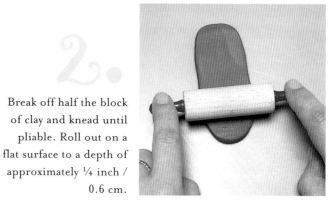

Break off half the block of clay and knead until pliable. Roll out on a flat surface to a depth of approximately ¼ inch / 0.6 cm.

Draw your motif on cardboard and cut it out.

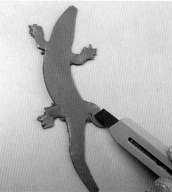

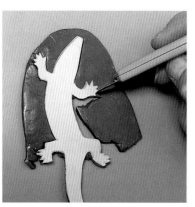

Place the cardboard template on top of the rolled-out clay. Carefully cut around the outline of the shape using the tip of the craft knife.

Clean up any ragged edges and go over details like the toes to get a perfect shape. (The edges of the clay can be smoothed with an emery board after baking.)

5.

Use the tip of a wooden skewer to texture the clay to look like crocodile skin and make indentations for the eyes.

6. Make two holes in the clay for the fastening pin—to ensure a perfect fit, see *Getting Started*.

7.

Fire the shape on an oven-proof curved surface, such as a mug. When cool, paint with a coat of varnish. Cut a length of copper wire approximately 6 inches / 15.2 cm long. Gently curve the wire and carefully insert through both holes. Test it in your hair and trim the copper wire to the right length. File the tip smooth or cover with a tight fitting bead—pad the hole with a piece of rubber if it is loose. Finish by gluing the emerald crystal eyes in place.

Variations on a Theme

Strips of different colored clays were pressed into the surface of this plain fish base. A coat of varnish intensifies the color and gives the barrette a glossy sheen (right).

A pretty butterfly is easy to cut from brightly-colored clay. The body and detail on the wing tips were added using separate pieces of clay (far right).

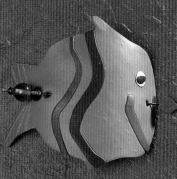

Acknowledgments

Grateful thanks to the many people without whose help and support this book would not have been published. First and most important, to my parents for their endless patience and for turning a blind eye when I used their home as a design studio. To Lindsey Stock and Jackie Schou for their additional design ideas, and to Paul Forrester for his creative photography. And, finally, to Shawna Mullen and Martha Wetherill, who made sense of everything I have written and gave valuable support and encouragement when times got tough.

About the Author

Jo Moody is a journalist who specializes in fashion and craft, and who has spent many years working for women's magazines. She is now a freelance stylist and writer, contributing features and designs to a variety of publications. Her childhood fascination with jewelry has developed into a passion—she loves rediscovering traditional crafts and using them in new ways to transform everyday things into truly beautiful jewelry.

Index

Sketch your ideas ...